"For my wife Najet and children, Haydan, Nahil, and Zeina, You are my reason. Love, Dad." — S.T.

www.SygaThomas.com

Printed in the United States of America

Book design and illustrations by Ben Lew

First Edition: 2022

This book is not intended to be a source of financial advice. Making adjustments to a financial strategy or plan should only be undertaken after consulting with a professional. The publisher and the author make no guarantee of financial results obtained by using this book.

Save, Spend, Share

Budgeting for Kids!

By: Syga Thomas

Illustrated By: Ben Lew

For Grown-ups

How can we teach young children to develop and maintain healthy financial habits? Save, Spend, Share: Budgeting for Kids! aims to help children understand that money is for more than just buying toys—it is for saving, spending, and sharing with others. With this resource in hand, parents can introduce smart financial practices in a way that speaks to kids using joyful illustrations and age-appropriate language. Financial concepts in the book include:

- **The difference between needs versus wants**
- **How to earn money**
- **The reasons to save money**
- **Selfishness versus selflessness with money**
- **Other ways to give, such as time and talents**
- **How having money requires responsibility**

Use this book to establish the basics of money management with your children and build a foundation that will last a lifetime.

Save, Spend, Share

Budgeting for Kids!

Money is funny.
Money can grow!
If you plant a penny,
How high will it go?

Will it wiggle and waggle
across your backyard?
Or soar like a rocket into the stars?

Will it fall from a flower
like petals to grass?

Or appear in your wallet
and turn into cash?

No! Money is *earned*.
That's how it grows!
It's earned when you work.
That's how it goes.

You may work for a boss or work on your own.
The money you earn has three cornerstones –

Save,

Spend,

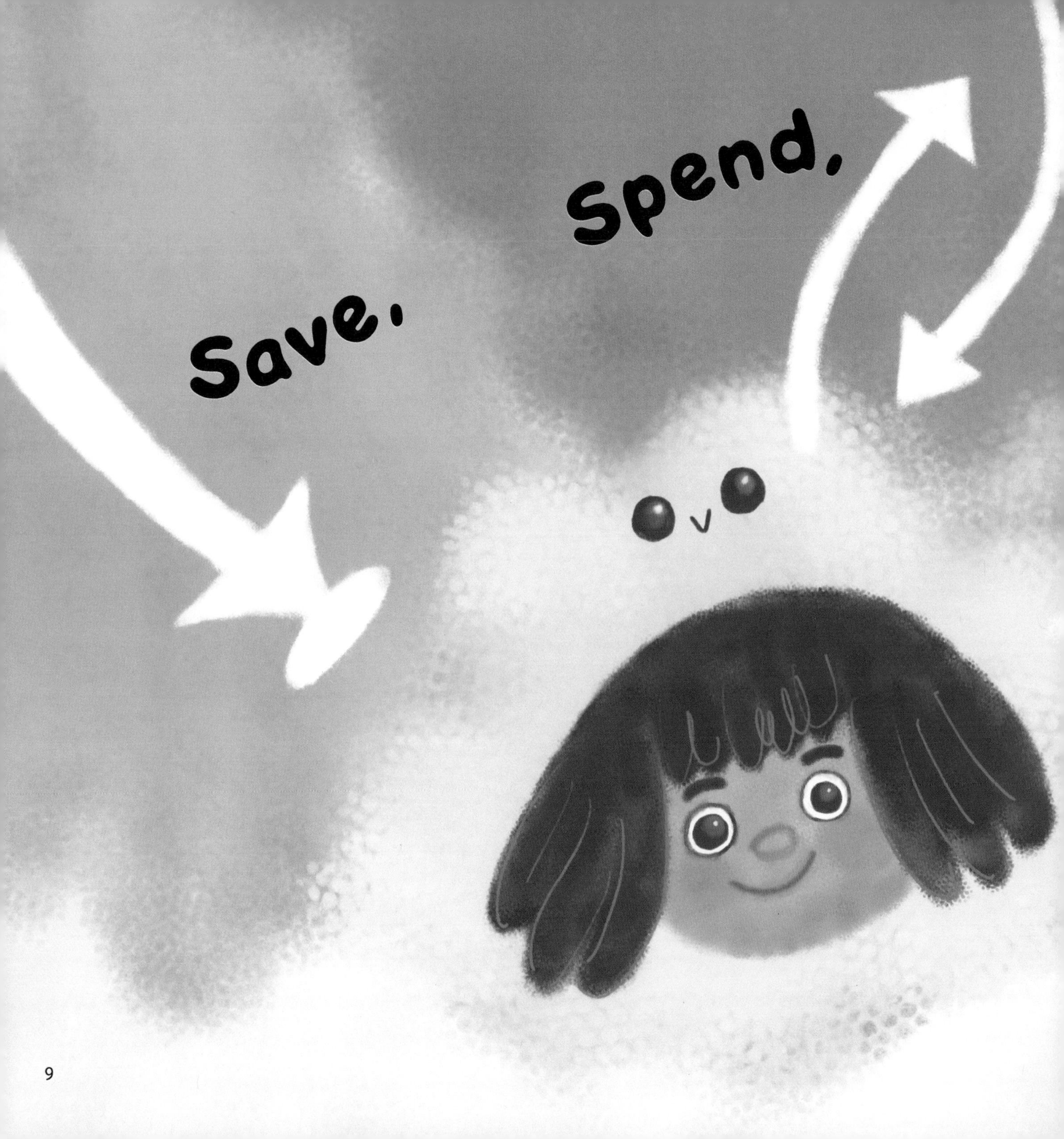

Share!

In time, you will see:

If you care for your money, you will be free.

Free to have fun,
Free to help others.
Free to make pennies
turn into dollars.

Save means you keep it.
Spend means you use it.
Share means you give it.
All three means YOU DID IT!

12

You could go to the store,
Buy a tablet or doll,
There are both needs and wants,
and you can't have it all.

A need you must have.
A want you would like.
A need and a want are nothing alike.

Spending your money is like eating a snack.
Once it is gone, it doesn't come back!

You could spend all your dough,
but saving is key!
There are lots of reasons to
save your money.

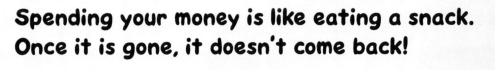

Saving takes time.
Saving takes courage.
Someday your savings
could send you to college.

College could send you
down into the sea,
Up into space,
Or to the army.

You could start your own business,
Or win a debate.
Or learn how to manage the money you make!

If you have saved wisely,
And have a nice stash,
When someone needs money,
You could help in a flash!

Emergencies come fast,
Like a simple mistake.
Like dropping the pan
When baking a cake.

Or popping a tire.
Or starting a fire.
Or running and tripping over a wire.

The future YOU might need money too.
What you save now could come to the rescue!

Charity is giving your
Time,
Talent,
Treasure.

Charity is truly a
superpower.

When you give:
You get stronger,
You shine brighter,

20

You feel better,
You are prouder,
You stay kinder,
You rise higher,
Forever.

Giving is thoughtful, no
matter the number.
Just a few dollars could
make things much better.

But if you remember just ONE thing somehow,
Think about what I will say now.

Money is good, but people are better.
Money can help, but love is the answer.

A mountain of dollars won't make you happy.
Without love in your heart, money is empty.

Whining and stomping,
Nagging and huffing,
Don't let a few dollars
make you demanding.

Use earnings responsibly,
Hold your head high.
The right use of money will unify.

Save, spend, and *share* –
keep these in your head.

And when you make money,
recall what you've read!

Author: Syga Thomas is an entrepreneur and personal finance expert. After receiving his graduate degree in International Economics from Johns Hopkins University, he spent several years abroad with the U.S. Department of State as an Economic Officer learning about effective investing.

Having left the public sector, Syga now spends his time coaching personal finance, wealth management, and healthy money habits. His energetic lessons on his YouTube channel and Go Money podcast aim to teach Americans the financial literacy skills he wishes were taught in school.

A passionate teacher and philanthropist, Syga's favorite professional endeavors are those that lead to the betterment of individuals and communities - and now, children. He resides in Washington D.C. with his wife and three children.

Illustrator: Ben Lew is a designer and illustrator who loves to make things for kids. When he's not doing that he's usually making things with his kids, strumming a guitar or ukulele, and thinking about video games. His favorite ninja turtle is Donatello but the quizzes always say he's Mikey.

Printed in Great Britain
by Amazon